香港國際詩歌之夜 2013
INTERNATIONAL POETRY NIGHTS IN HONG KONG

編輯 Editors

北島 Bei Dao

陳嘉恩 Shelby K. Y. Chan

方梓勳 Gilbert C. F. Fong

柯夏智 Lucas Klein

馬德松 Christopher Mattison

添姆・利爾本
Tim Lilburn

目錄 Contents

1 Past Jordan River

A Traveler, who is Odysseus, wandering among ferns

Loss Creek, near the coast,
Scythes its polished wheat shovel at Leech River fault
Slewing bushels of quartz-like self-substantia,
Small, cut-faced berries of itself,
Quickly
Under the singlelane, railway
Tie bridge. In birdlessness.
Moments later a tarry flux
Handstands and cannons
Through the rub-silvered barrel of its own body
Five hundred feet over Sombrio beach.
The water drops, it tears.
Alders on the bank
Like crushed asphalt.

Out of clearcut dusk, bears,
One, then another,
Take the ridge,
Dipping down.

(From *Assiniboia*)

喬丹河那邊

旅行者奧德修斯獨自在蕨草間盤桓

失落澗，近海岸
鐮刀霍霍，光潤的麥子推倒向荔池河斷層
屠宰他們石英般的豐富自在，
顆顆谷粒晶瑩如漿果
飛快地
倒在鐵路的單行道邊
吊橋，鳥雀不來的安靜
片刻之後鐵流奔湧
倒立蜻蜓和加農炮
穿過磨光鋥亮的炮膛林立
桑布里奧海灘蜿蜒五百呎
水落如滴淚
岸上的阿德斯平原
彷佛壓碎的瀝青

黎明清晰的晨光中，黑熊出沒
一隻，又一隻
佔領山脊
順坡而下

（摘自《阿西尼波埃》，謝凌嵐譯）

2 Bull's Forehead Hill

Narrator, his voice pebble on pebble, rolling down a grade

Two thousand pound hill with a gigantic cock. Times
A few hundred thousand. Teeming, dolphin
Necked, patched with a sand saddle, deuce of rivers
Cable link into each other's rattler's jaws in front
Of it, runaway
Current sand slab downshifting against the bluff,
Then mooching east. A heron works
The dusk, crackle of shadows.
Antelope.

(From *Assiniboia*)

牛首山

講述者，他的聲音象鵝卵石滾山坡

兩千磅的山坡乘以幾十萬，長出一個大雞巴
河岔密集如海豚交頸
沙洲星羅棋佈
犬牙交互
脱韁之馬
大浪淘沙，在懸崖峭壁前至步
再掉頭東去。蒼鷺穿行暮色
萬箭穿心夜幕
是羚羊

（摘自《阿西尼波埃》，謝凌嵐譯）

3 **Island**

The Traveler

Rattling undercarriage of geese over this rainmound
shed,
Its smell of burning heater dust like drying barley,
Swampy walls held in a crib of whale jaw bone.
Fish punch into these walls, digging in
On night's paleo-currents.
Their eggs have been found in certain human ears.
November thump of salmon
Hums all rock.
Flickers thicken the dogwood
With shaking, stabbing their three cornered fruit.
The woman-archon comes, pollened with intelligence,
Each second or third dawn, lays her cigarette on the
bedside table,
Ash end out, draws back the sheet
And lowers her face.
Warm afternoons, to get free of the flu
Of rain, I worm into caves;
Greased hat of bats, grime shine of their skins;

Their ammonia smell almost rubs me out.
Driftwood slides off every form
I make on the beach, the tide takes it, I'll never leave.
Vines, violets, springs; a band tightens around this
head.
Someone breathes down a flute needle rasped into
swan wing bone,
Another has twisted coat hangers around
Bear shoulder blades and slices these through fires
To dog what speech splits across those lofts
Of white heave near his eye.
The marks say I won't leave.
Icebergs appear in the bays, waddling through the
Spanish names.
Turkey vultures swim up
Over slab crests of stub mountains.

(From *Assiniboia*)

島嶼

漫遊者

野鵝縱隊帶著震顫的底盤飛越雨水濕透的茅舍
氣味像加熱器上的灰塵又像烘乾的大麥
鯨魚下齶殘骸四壁長滿水草
魚在其中埋漕產卵
夜裏的古生代暗流
有人可以聽見這些魚卵剝落而至
十一月的三文魚群
讓所有的岩石哼唱
山茱萸樹枝條搖弋
每一次搖動都在穿刺他們三角形的果實
智慧傳授花粉，由古代的女祭祀完成
在次第的黎明，把她手裏的香煙放在床頭小桌上
煙灰向外，和衣而臥
把她的臉深埋進被褥
待溫暖的午後，為逃避流感
逃避雨，我鑽入洞穴
蝙蝠油膩的帽頂，帶黏液的皮膚閃著微光
他們氨水一樣的體息讓我暈眩
浮木形狀各異

我終於到達沙灘，海潮漸至，我將永不離開
藤籮、紫羅蘭和清泉是緊箍咒
吹氣如蘭，笛孔裏的呼吸變作天鵝之翼骨
另一口氣扭曲衣架，套進
熊的肩胛骨，一併掠過火焰
高頻音撕裂屋脊，
眉骨間堆白
那個刺青説決不離開
海灣裏出現冰山，在西班牙語的地名間搖擺
山鷹逆流而上
飛過絕壁的山頂

（摘自《阿西尼波埃》，謝凌嵐譯）

4 Exegesis

The Stranger, who is Dionysos

Milkweed, milkweed, soft-toothed moons
burbling saxophonic inside; within, rising pastures
and cow bells,
milkweed, beside broken greenhouses of rivers,
  milkweed.
Milkweed, dissolved, re-skeletoned
with the sun's horned current,
milkweed, in itself, leap-igniting
as 31 year old Cyd Charisse in *The Band Wagon*
with the shark-chewed Fred Astaire, 1953.
In milkweed a pole of liturgically clothed cats, then
behind this, the palace with breasted pillars,
where everyone is heard.
The *ta' wil* of milkweed,
that machinery, is caress and proferring ambassadorial
  gifts.
The milkweed holds still, holds still
for the eschatologically optimistic hermeneutic of
  milkweed,

milkweed, in the mind of Joseph, sitting beside
  milkweed
near the path, dream-taxonomist, sizzling
eye-balcony in the electron microscope theatre
—milkweed is the campaigns of Alexander into India.
It is a feeding station setting out bowls
of meat and bowls of rice for the children of the town
  of Blairmore, Alberta.
Pillar of ideograms.
The books are laid out, the gold lettering appears.
In milkweed hangs a coat of chainmail from the
  Crusades
sewn by crying spiders.
The table is set, gold letters appear.
Milkweed, flowering yellow, with black beauty marks,
milkweed, milkweed, by the throaty, overcome,
  Romeoric greenhouses of rivers
that gruff and mood and lord their load of tonnes
of cut flowers of shadow further east, north then east.

(From *Assiniboia*)

釋經篇

陌生人，他是酒神狄奧尼索斯

乳草，乳草，葉圓如月
乳草裏升起一個草原，瑟瑟如薩克斯管的鳴奏
還有牛鈴
乳草，河邊殘牆斷垣邊的乳草
在太陽光線的金箭下
枝葉四散的乳草
自燃自燒
三十一歲的塞德・夏里斯自《大篷車》一舉成名
與她同道的是被鯊魚咬過的富萊德・阿斯特爾，
　　1953 年
茂盛參天，立著雷紋龍形的山貓圖騰柱
在它的後面，帶華表的宮殿
眾神皆在傾聽
乳草之尾
那柔韌的機器，撫摸和兼作外交禮物
風欲靜，乳草的枝葉靜止
以樂觀末世論來解構乳草的涵義
在聖徒約瑟夫的腦海裏，乳草邊坐著
臨近道路的是夢的分類學家，灼熱燃燒

電子的小宇宙在眼簾裏波動
——乳草茂盛如亞歷山大出征印度
擺滿一碗碗魚肉米飯的餐車
給阿爾伯塔省布萊梅爾鎮的孩子們
表意文字的巨擘
聖書已經打開，書頁上的金字閃閃爍爍
乳草上披掛著十字軍的傳銷信
密佈如衣裳由蛛絲織就

盛宴的餐桌擺出了，金色的字母顯現
乳草盛開黃花，長著美人痣
乳草，乳草，漫山遍野地征服河邊羅密歐式的溫室
山巒河汊，佔地為王，千里為疆
黃花遍地一路向東，向北再轉戰向東

（摘自《阿西尼波埃》，謝淩嵐譯）

譯註：

賽德・夏里斯是美國1950年代著名演員、舞蹈家，以電影《雨中曲》和《大篷車》的表演揚名好萊塢。

5 He Announces His Devotion to Sara Riel, Her Theurgical Action

The Stranger

1879 or thereabouts, 1882, a back way opened behind
  the actual
Years, water pushed under and through glacier ice,
And down it, elongated, Hudson Bay drainage long
  priesthole,
Twohandedly, you lance forward a platter made of horn
On which reclines a volcano highrise, tipping,
  curtseying, of fruit,
No, wait, sorry, wait, better light
In the hall and the room you've just entered,
I see it firmer now, a bowl, sleeping
Putto of lung blood.
The well-fleshed, kneading, draped place,
Shack in the woods, in the claws of the trees,
In the throat of the trees, chimney-shaped, that house,
You go in.
The blood's a red bush now
And at its foot nesting quail.

You make this entrance,
Twice your size with feathers, insistent,
With precise, ludic feet
Often.
This is how you think.
The room, underseen, bricked away,
Quakes around its oil lamp,
Three days ride north of prairie,
Here the spin of the world is cleaned;
Prie-dieued, one eyed by a steel crucifix, buffalo herd
Coat shag of lamped shadow, squeezing, bulking,
pulling back.
Your room.
Snow racks down like a canyon wall
At Ile a La Crosse,
A snowmobile tilts back, fires on a spinal tread,
To bite toward the fixed
Core of a lake,
Headbeam swaying.
Across again the room, you haul

—no choir to carry it voicely,
no choir—
And haul
A century of never-unmoving, fat-marbled hair.

(From *Assiniboia*)

他宣佈皈依塞拉・里爾，膜拜她的神通之能

陌生人

大約在1879年至1882年間，闢徑開通
河水在冰川下流過，
河水之下，哈得遜灣的三角洲在悄然伸展，
雙手著地，你雀躍向前，落在號角的盤上
水果累累，堆積如岌岌可危的火山之塔
哦不，請等下，請等下更亮的光線
在你剛剛走進的房間
我看見，清晰可見，一隻碗
靜如睡眠，碗中咳血
深藏於林，簾幕重重的地方
在樹的魔爪下
這煙囪形狀的房子
你走進來
紅色的灌木如血
斑鳩築巢其中
你舉足進門
巨大的雙足帶著羽毛，步履堅定
步伐精確

時常
這就是你的想像之足
那間看不見的房間，磚石所壘
地基在油燈之下震動
在大平原之北飛馳三天三夜
世界之軸，被打磨清洗
獨眼的十字架，駕馭野牛的群隊
燈光的陰影如蓑衣襤褸，轉動，搖晃，抽身而退
你的房間
雪落下垂直如絕壁
在十字島上

電動雪橇傾斜，在螺旋的雪道上打出火花
咬住那湖心
凝固的內核
車前燈搖晃
來回照亮房間，你拖拉拽動
——唱不成合唱
唱不成歌——

無人拖動
一世紀來從未動過的沾滿油脂的毛髮

（摘自《阿西尼波埃》，謝凌嵐譯）

6 Beyond Jordan River, Going

Our Lord Odysseus, the Traveler, timekeeping, rising,
taking his shape from the cauldron of his calculations

Origen, Origen, out of Alexandria, confused, afflicted
in the fir,
Foreign ears cloved to him,
Bears and Origen out of decayed day clear cut
Achieve the ridge, November bears, sudden black door
of them
Studded with blow-whitened spikeheads of alertness,
Dipping down,
And they intercept the nineteenth century.
Origen works an exegesis down to its skeleton,
Dragon of the years,
And slides in a word like a titanium rod.
John Climacus and his trembling ladder of
lamentation. Weep.
Origen, armored with his upper arm of eyes,
Origen, made a seal by hearing.
There's a white volcano across the water; it's
immediately keen

And leans in. Look back. The Industrial Revolution
Colored creek drops and tears.

Alders on a bank like crushed asphalt.
The creek, an antibiotic coma,
Someone reciting the names of everyone
Who lived in a completely burned city.

(From *Assiniboia*)

穿過喬丹河，繼續行進

我主奧德修斯，旅行者，即時而起，從他的思考之鼎中升起

奧利金，亞歷山大城來的奧利金，已經轉暈
飽受折磨後，異形的耳朵在他頭上支起
熊和奧利金從草場走出
走上山脊，十一月的熊，黑色的穿越之門開啟
他們敏銳如淬火後白色的箭鏃
向下
他們攔截了十九世紀
奧利金在苦修經卷
年代久遠的龍
出沒詞彙之林彷彿鈦金之杖
約翰·克萊門喀斯顫抖哭泣，在神的梯子邊
奧利金，上臂長眼全副武裝，
奧利金，耳聞千里，聽覺可以密封書信
水中的白火山，忽然啟動
靠近，回望，工業革命已經到來
多彩的小溪跌落四散

安德斯平原在河岸上伸展如壓碎的瀝青
溪水裏是抗生素的昏迷
有人在叫每個人的名字
每個曾在焚毀之城生活過的人的名字

（摘自《阿西尼波埃》，謝凌嵐譯）

譯註：

1. 奧利金在埃及的亞歷山大城出生和傳教，是早期基督教的主要思想家，著述頗豐，後因與羅馬教廷的教義分歧而被目為異類。
2. 約翰・克萊門喀斯是7 世紀基督教聖徒。

7 **Black Hut**

The black hut, outlined in blue, the voice,
Backs into the forest, Gershom Scholem's
Major Trends rides its desk,
Floating, abetting the dream unit.
Snow has only just disappeared. Exhausted light,
Light that's come through surgery and its superb
Mini-bar of morphine coils in the window,
Tough, or obsessed, curl Clerk Maxwell's
Displacement current egged, phished, straightforwardly
Begged to stipple in nothing. It's here and loaded.
The fruitless pear tree near bloom in cold
Grows an inch forward, first instants
Of originary inflation replayed. One of its branches
Rakes the roof.
Adonis says *The innards of matter come toward me.*
They do, they walk as if they knew
The body they moved in was Hector Berlioz's
Symphony Fantastic, Leonard Bernstein's version, 1968.
  Or
The True Spirit and Original Intent of Treaty 7.

黑色茅屋

黑色茅屋輪廓呈現藍色的剪影，聲音響起
回森林去，這是吉襄施隆的聲音
*特蘭德上校*騎坐在書桌上
在水上漂流，一邊循循善誘
雪剛剛消失，把光線耗盡
光線從手術室透過來，它又超凡地，
聚光在窗戶上的嗎啡小酒櫃
堅持不懈的克拉克·麥克斯韋爾磁場
放電電流一往無前
請求在虛空中點畫，陽光在此，飽滿厚重
穀底的梨樹只開花不結果，寒冷中
向前生長一寸，最初的瞬間
破芽萌發的瞬間一再重現，一根枝條
穿破屋脊
阿多尼斯説，*事物的內臟朝我走來*
千真萬確，他們彷彿認識路一般地向我走來
他們換了一副皮囊，進入海克特·博利奧茲的身體
絕妙交響曲，利奧納多·伯恩斯坦的1968年指揮
　　版本

真正的精神，以及第7號協議之原旨

（謝凌嵐譯）

譯註：

1. 吉襄施隆是當代猶太學者，是首位研究卡巴拉神秘主義教派的學者。
2. 克拉克·麥克斯韋爾，英國理論物理學家，電磁場理論開創人。

8 Exempla

1

Someone has returned from the dead
And wears a stone-weighted, stretched, blue coat
Decorated with equations and nouns in Arabic and
   Latin
Stitched in white thread along its arms, both the tops
And under and from the shoulders to the knee.
The words and numbers slant and cross each other
On the outside and up and down the inner lining.
When he fully opens the panes of this coat,
You can see fire moving in a circular current
On his body, downward toward his feet then into grass
And into wet ground where it begins
A return upward and enters him again
Through the top of his head.
Clinkers arc from this fire and perforate
The hands of anyone watching.

2

The young man has seen something
And refuses now to speak.

He hides in the wounds of the mountain,
Its gorings
And won't come down below the snow to calls.
He saw the man standing in the choir,
Blood fountaining from his eyes and ears.
The young man's complete body shook in the act
Of hearing at that moment.
It whipped in the taste, a single alert organ.
The curl of wood bucked jerkily
From the cross and pinned him between its arms.
Below he sees the tips of pines move and notes
The smell coming off snow.

3

In the room of Selo of Wilton, the shield comes
Out of curtains of dark and reflects
The late 12th century face
Of the syllogistic master at Oxford.
In the midst of the gruff glow
Of the nubbly surface, bobbing on the reflected face,
  another

Mouth floats from the metal and speaks
Through the layer of the face
In the room's frost.
Master Selo's time is short, his years vain.
A fire burns, snapping in the room.
The master's dead student, nude, appeared
Two nights ago, with even his skin removed
By the whip of thin weapons.
Lipless, he quivered in hatred
Of argument.
No one tonight holds the shield that cups
The soft candle of the teacher's face.
Here is the spur of true philosophy.
Ether stirs in the room, a throaty wisp,
As the metal thing passes through it.

成例

一

有人從冥界返回
皂色長褸，石頭鑲邊
裝飾著阿拉伯語和拉丁語的警句
衣角領子鑲白
從肩至膝
文字縱橫交錯
從裏到外遍佈衣裳
當他打開長袍的夾襯
可見火焰旋動
在他身體上自上往下，火焰從足上跳至足下之草
火焰燃進濕地，
然後火焰再起，周而復始
至燒到他的發頂
火焰一路燒得劈啪作響，
把旁觀者的手燒出窟窿

二

年輕人已經看見什麼
但拒絕說出
他躲進群山的傷口

它的內傷
他不離不棄就不下山
他看見合唱隊裏那個人
耳目出血神形可怖
年輕人全身戰慄，受驚過度
當他聽說那人受難的一刻
鞭打味覺，唯一的報警器官
木頭上的倒刺逆向而生
十字架把他的雙臂釘住
朝下望去，他看見松樹之巔在顫動
腥味自雪上飄來

三

居於威爾頓的賽洛，巨大的盾牌送至他的房間
自黑幕後面，映現
十二世紀末期的臉
牛津語音大師的臉
氤氳於粗糙的輝光
盾牌糙面折光，鏡面的臉虛像點點
另一張嘴，在發號施令
在重重疊疊的虛像中

在房間裹的霜霧裹
賽洛大師時日無多，功虧一簣
點起火，火舌在房間裹繚繞
大師已逝的弟子裸體顯現
兩天前，他被處削刑
體無完膚
連嘴唇都被割掉，
他在異見的仇恨裹顫抖
今夜，無人舉起真理的盾牌
蠟燭熔化是大師的臉
此刻的哲學之道
以瑟攪動房間裹的空氣，發出喉音
當金屬穿牆而過

（謝凌嵐譯）

9 Nature

I am trying to read the form of longing
And see a wind with the sun inside it
Coming out of the east, 6:45 am,
Moving across the campus where I have a room
For a few days, in the south part of the city,
Near the ring road and flooded fields past that.
A small moon earlier, around five,
In a fog of distance, over mowed grass in the
quadrangle.

All conscious life (says the *Summa
Contra Gentiles*) streams to throw its bright rope
Around the torso of God, or seeds
In the mind of God or the necks
Of dolphins in the mind of God.

960 Garnet, the aunts, uncles, parents
Sitting around two card tables, late
In the Fifties, tumblers of rye and ginger in their
hands,
War over, eating bridge mix, Planter's nuts,

Cards expertly shuffled and dealt.
All with cigarettes, unfiltered, mentholed,
The men in jackets, one without in braces and shirt
   band,
Each in shined shoes, the women in nylons.
Their laughter whippy with sexual crest,
They wave their cigarettes as they argue
Their hands and tease and quickly,
Now and then like birds feeding, touch one another,
Shoulders and wrists.
Around midnight the women bring out
Lunch—sandwiches, coffee, fruitcake—as if
Beating another thin wall of gold
To one already there.
The winter outside, hideously wide
Ford engine blocks sink and clot in frost.
There is a carefully flaked and notched
Brown flint point from the Avonlea Culture
Lost under three layers of light
In air near them, then a little farther on,

A chip of corded, grey pottery from Old Woman's
  Culture
Lies on its side on a slope of some brilliant tilth.
They wave their cigarettes in the gold churn of air,
Kids ducking under the swooping blobs of ember,
Shoot back their heads, showing teeth and howl.

自然

我試圖讀出渴望的形式
於是看見風挾裹著一顆太陽
自東而來，早上6點45分
風吹過我住的校園
風吹了幾天，在城南
靠近環路和洪水淹過的田地
一輪薄月在下午五點升起
遠遠起霧了，霧彌漫過新割草的庭院
所有自在自覺的生活
都把一道亮麗的繩索
套在上帝的身上，湯瑪斯·阿圭那的《真理論》如
　　是說
上帝之眼裏，虔誠的種子，
對等海豚的脖子

加內德街960號，叔舅姑嫂，父母雙親
濟濟圍坐兩張牌桌
五十年代末，裸麥和生薑飲料在手
戰爭結束，吃橋牌零食，椒鹽花生
洗牌發牌手法嫻熟

不帶濾嘴的薄荷味的香煙在手
男人西裝革履，或者發帶手鐲嬉皮打扮
皮鞋鋥亮，女人們穿尼龍衫
調笑聲與欲望同波
爭論時手中香煙搖搖欲墜
他們手勢複雜，諧戲有度
時不時互相碰觸，如鳥啄食
肩膀和手腕
半夜時女人們拿出午餐
三明治，咖啡和水果糕
打破黃金的薄牆
對於那個已經來到的人
冬天在門外，窮凶極惡的福特車寬闊的引擎
堵塞水池，在霧裏梗塞
片狀和齒狀的打火石排列緊密
來自於傳説中的阿文里鎮
在三層光線裏迷失
離他們不遠的空氣裏
是灰色的彩陶殘片，來自古老的母系社會
在肥沃的耕地上四散

他們支著香煙的手在空氣裏劃出金圈
孩子們把頭埋進餘燼之中
然後把頭仰起，露齒長嚎

（謝淩嵐譯）

譯註：

1. 湯瑪斯・阿圭那，中世紀基督教最重要的理論家、哲學家。
2. 阿文里鎮是加拿大著名兒童小説《綠色房子裏的安娜》裏的虛構小鎮。

10 Newton, Force at a Distance, Imperialism

The one waitress, in spiky *sotto voce*
To the bearded owner behind the coffee shop counter
About some cranky bill keeps saying
16.65, 16.65? And I think
Important year for Newton, Fluxions, etc.,
Theory of Colors, gravity growing
To the orb of the moon. Gold River, Muchalaht Inlet,
The rocks in these empty parts, because of
Their loneliness, even misanthropy,
Are giant, principal warehouses of the Lucasian
Professor's Force; they horde their plates of theorems,
Locked drawers of stresses.
The moon makes an appearance,
Whales move off the coast.
The Gold River Liquor Express, open seven days a
 week—
It's the density, the unreadable, mid-brain pull
From the rocks that oppresses the residents in the
 town,
Jacks them from furniture into their trucks
And down the hill, where they achieve the walk

Through the barred doors.
The coffee shop sits in a bowl of white peaks.
Nuu-chah-nulth First Nation, three times moved,
  hangs among trees
In a tight, rising canyon to the northwest
And never comes to town.
The town dreams a giant incinerator
In the abandoned pulpmill, burning Vancouver's
  garbage
Barged to it through night,
Diesel thump above the click of rain.

牛頓，遠控力量，帝國主義

一個女招待，在輕聲軟語
對咖啡館櫃檯後面的滿臉于思的掌櫃説，
關於幾張難纏的帳單，不停嘮叨
16.65, 16.65 ？我當成
牛頓生平重要的一年，微積分
光譜理論，引力生成？
還有月球公轉。黃金河，穆察拉哈特灣
岩石在這些空曠之地，孤絕
因此憎恨人類
憎恨盧卡斯那些巨無霸的貨倉
教授的引力，能叫他們把理論的盤子拿住
鎖上心煩意亂的抽屜
月亮偶顯真容
鯨魚游離海岸
黃金河烈酒專營店，一周七天開門營業
壓迫小鎮居民的力，無名無蹤，醍醐灌頂
來自岩石
把他們從傢俱邊拋向卡車
推下山坡，在那裏居民學會行走
走過緊閉的大門

咖啡館如在碗中，白色的群山是碗邊
努查努第一國家，三搬三遷，現在定居樹間
在一道西北向逼窄的峽谷中
從未回來
小鎮夢見一個巨大焚化爐
立於廢棄的紙漿廠，焚化溫哥華的垃圾
船運日夜不停
柴油發動機轟鳴，雨水錚錚作響

（謝凌嵐譯）

11 **Oh**

Living in the truck west
of Lake Cowichan, past the Youbou turn,
you know it, almost at the coast,
in the bloom of sleeping
bag and charcoal, back quiet in straight-sided valleys,
walking, poking around with a stick, in clearcut and
slash,
I am one of the first to meet winter coming
off the great water
and give her my name which disappears
inside.
Etienne Gilson on St. Bernard's mystical theology,
book of lips and breath,
top maps, I soft-mouthed exegete, parking receipts and
one
black banana on the dash and also passenger side floor.
Coho are just beginning to taste
the fan of fresh water
at the tip of the creeks,
eagles slide three hundred miles toward the rivers'
emptying mouths.

I slot whatever else there is to say into reed-shuffle at
  Lizard Lake.
Cold coming off the morning moon,
oak leaves, you could imagine, are turning purple black
down in the big place of Victoria.

哦

居住在卡車裏，
寇未蟬湖以西，尤伯屯再過去
你知道的，幾乎到達海岸
在熙熙攘攘的睡袋和木炭之間
回到筆直的山谷
手持樹棍四處走走，空地和溪澗
我是最早遭遇冬天的人
冬天來自於遼闊的水上
向冬天自我介紹，它卻遍尋不著
在伊坦尼吉布森的內心，聖徒伯納德的神秘主義書頁
嘴唇和呼吸的書頁
還有地圖，我輕聲解釋，近旁是停車費收據和一隻腐黑的香蕉
在駕駛副座
寇河三文魚回游
嘗到一絲淡水的滋味
在河水入海的扇形處
鷹擊水三百里，河谷空空
我把所思所想寫在蘆葦上，蘆葦投入湖裏

晨月帶來寒冷
橡樹葉變成紫黑色
在這個叫維多利亞的地方

(謝凌嵐譯)

添姆·利爾本生於加拿大薩斯喀徹溫省首府里賈納，至今出版了九本詩集，包括《河》(1999)、《殺戮場景》(2003) 及《神秘政治》(2008)。利爾本獲獎無數，一度榮獲「薩斯喀徹溫省年度書籍獎」及「加拿大作家協會獎」，《殺戮場景》更勇奪「加拿大總督獎」。利爾本的部分詩作輯錄於艾莉森·卡爾德所編的《慾望永在：添姆·利爾本詩選》(2007)。利爾本曾出版兩本論文集：《生存在世，猶如在家》(1999) 及《回家》(2008)，探討詩學、愛慾與政治，尤其關注環境論。他亦是論文集《詩學及知識》及《想像和歌唱：詩歌及哲學實踐》的編輯兼撰文者，兩本論文集均對詩學影響深遠。此外，他相信基督教的默想傳統或有助去殖民化，故曾大篇幅撰文論述柏拉圖和其他倡導默想傳統的思想家，如約翰·卡西安及《不明之雲》的作家。利爾本曾於加拿大西安大略大學、阿爾伯塔大學、聖瑪麗大學及里賈納公共圖書館當駐校作家，現於維多利亞大學寫作系任教。利爾本的作品獲翻譯成不同語言，並編成文集。他的最新著作為三幕咏歎《阿西尼波埃》，當中選段得到加拿大數家當代舞蹈團改編成舞蹈表演。

（黃凱嵐譯）

Tim Lilburn was born in Regina, Saskatchewan. He has published nine books of poetry, including *To the River* (1999), *Kill-site* (2003), and *Orphic Politics* (2008). His work has received Canada's Governor General's Award (for *Kill-site*), the Saskatchewan Book of the Year Award, and the Canadian Authors Association Award among other prizes. A selection of his poetry is collected in *Desire Never Leaves: The Poetry of Tim Lilburn* (Wilfird Laurier University Press, 2007), edited by Alison Calder. Lilburn has produced two books of essays, both concerned with poetics, eros and politics, especially environmentalism: *Living in the World As If It Were Home* (1999) and *Going Home* (2008). He has also edited and contributed to two influential essay anthologies on poetics, namely *Poetry and Knowing* and *Thinking and Singing: Poetry and the Practice of Philosophy*. He has written at length on Plato and thinkers in the Christian contemplative tradition, such as John Cassian and the author of *The Cloud of Unknowing*, in the belief that a resuscitation of this tradition may have a decolonizing effect. Lilburn has been a writer-in-residence at the University of Western Ontario, the University of Alberta and St. Mary's University, as well as the Regina Public Library, and now teaches in the Department of Writing at the University of Victoria. His work has been widely translated and anthologized. His most recent book is *Assiniboia*, an opera for chant in three parts, sections of which have been choreographed and performed by contemporary dance companies in Canada.

出版 Publisher
香港中文大學出版社 The Chinese University Press

封面影像 Cover Image
北島 Bei Dao

出版日期 Date of Publication
二零一三年十一月 November 2013

國際書號 ISBN
978-962-996-616-4

香港國際詩歌之夜 2013 International Poetry Nights in Hong Kong 2013
主辦單位 Organizers
香港中文大學文學院 Faculty of Arts, The Chinese University of Hong Kong
香港浸會大學文學院 Faculty of Arts, Hong Kong Baptist University
香港科技大學人文社會科學學院 School of Humanities and Social Science, The Hong Kong University of Science and Technology

合作夥伴 In Partnership With
英國文化協會 British Council

協辦單位 Co-organizers
時刻文化 Moment Communications
香港中文大學出版社 The Chinese University Press

贊助 Sponsors
香港兆基創意書院 HKICC Lee Shau Kee School of Creativity
中國會 The China Club
周凱旋基金會 Chau Hoi Shuen Foundation

Printed in Hong Kong